To Merritt –

Phyllis Hillugs
May 16, 1997

A WEB OF GOOD MANNERS

Grown-up Manners for Young People

by Phyllis Hillings

Illustrated by John Louis Tegtmeyer

MANHATTAN PRESS

Pasadena, California

MANHATTAN PRESS
260 S. Lake Avenue, No. 222, Pasadena, CA 91101

Publisher's Cataloging in Publication
(Prepared by Quality Books Inc.)

Hillings, Phyllis K., 1925-
A web of good manners: grown-up manners for young people
Phyllis Hillings
p. cm.
Includes index.
Preassigned LCCN: 92-085125
Audience: Children eight years old and up
SUMMARY: A book of good manners and proper social behavior in
rhymed verse.
ISBN 0-9634642-1-3
1. Etiquette for children and teenagers--Juvenile verse.   2. Social skills in
children--Juvenile verse.   3. Etiquette. I. Title. II. Title: Grown-up
manners for young people.

BJ1857.C5H55 1993   395′.122
                                      QBI92-1214

This is for Pamela,
And Jennifer, and Dave,
About whom I'm always
So willing to rave.
I practiced on them,
Taught them all that I knew,
Took care of them, loved them,
And watched while they grew
To be young adults
With children of their own
Whom I now can teach
Since mine up all are grown.

ACKNOWLEDGEMENTS

I would first like to thank my ADVISORY BOARD who had the courtesy and took the time to respond to my questionnaire, counseling me on topics about which I am not as knowledgeable, such as what's "cool," and what's "NOT!"

They are: Ryan Brady (9), Alexandria, VA; Christopher Eastland (13), and Richard Eastland (15), Southport, CT; Bekah Ford (10) and Sarah Ford (13), Winston-Salem, NC; Peter Grech (13), Pasadena, CA; Lindsey Hess (9), Arcadia, CA; Jennifer Keatinge (13), Encinitas, CA; Libby Keatinge (13), Pacific Palisades, CA; Jason and Joshua Johnson (12-year-old twins), Pasadena, CA; Rady Large (11), Sylva, NC; Kelly Shaw (10), and Richard Shaw (12), Issaquah, WA, and Heather Vance (10) and Tyne Vance (12), Tulsa, OK.

Then I would like to thank my advisors who are older in years but so young in heart: Shirley Christensen, my sister who was my research person; Helene Drown who has been urging me to write a book for over a decade; Carol Finch, my grammarian; Ethel Jackson, always there to offer encouragement; Mary McAboy, the accomplished proof-reader; Kathy Monahan whose professional advice was always welcomed, and Judy Van Rest of Alexandria, VA, who so generously edited my book.

Special thanks go to my typesetter, Steve Harle, of Ross Typographic Service, Inc., who was such fun to work with and so patient with all my changes, and finally to John Tegtmeyer, my illustrator, my son-in-law, and still my friend.

Another special thanks to McDonald's for giving me permission to use its "Mc" for the chapter titled McManners.

If there are any errors in this book, I made them.....I did it MY WAY!

TABLE OF CONTENTS

TABLE OF CONTENTS (Con't)

PREFACE

You are never born with manners,
They are something you are taught,
And if your parents or teachers don't,
Then you really, truly ought
To read this book or take a class
In proper social behavior,
For when you're out there in the grown-up world,
That knowledge might be your savior.

So start right now, with the aid of this book,
To build your self-esteem,
And in a few years, there's no doubt at all
You could serve as Prom King or Prom Queen.

INTRODUCTION

Sit down boys and girls,
And I'll tell you a story
Of how to grow up
To greatness and glory.
But first you must learn about
"Thank you" and "Please"
And how to take care of that
Noisy, wet sneeze.

So just settle down
And let us begin,
For a web of good manners
Is starting to spin.....

CHAPTER I

INTRODUCTIONS

How to: How-Do-You-Do?

When introducing people,
Name the older person first;
Say, "Mr. Old, meet Mary Young,"
And you will not be cursed.
Then, "Mrs. Young, meet Robert Old,"
And add a word or two
To get a conversation going,
That's what you want to do.

When introducing a friend of yours,
You use the same technique,
Such as mention that you met in camp,
To give your friends a peek
At what type of subject would be good...
Tell how you rode a horse
So you can get the chatter started
And then leave without remorse.

If making introductions
When you're standing in a group,
Don't forget the one who's all alone,
Over there with his hula hoop.

ONE LEFT OUT

NO ONE LEFT OUT

Bring everyone in on the meeting
So no one will be left out;

To ignore someone in the greetings
Would be rude beyond a doubt.

For some silly, silly reason,
And I truly don't know why,
Your relatives are mentioned last,
Now isn't that kind of sly?
And anyone who has a title
Comes before all the rest,
Although in many cases
They are really far from best.

*   *   *   *   *   *

Remember to call
Your dearest friend's mother,
"Mrs. Brady," "Mrs. Byrnes," "Mrs. Laird,"
But no other.
She's never called "Kit,"
Or "Betty," or "Mary,"
And her father's not "John,"
Or "Donley," or "Jerry."

All older people are called
By their own last names,

And even if they're nice
And join in your games,
Don't <u>ever</u> forget
And say "Melvin," or "Burt,"
For your social standing
Might really get hurt.

About shaking hands
When you meet an adult,
Don't extend your hand first,
That's a little insult;
For you're just a kid
And not sure in your ways,
So let them extend first,
Grasp it firmly and say,
"Nice to meet you, Mrs. Robinson,
Have a nice day."
Smile cheerfully or nod,
Then be on your way.

* * * * * *

When your parents give a party
And introduce you to a guest,
Do you look him in the eye and smile
And really act your best?

Or do you squirm and shuffle
And look down at the floor
And hope it will be over soon.
It's such an awful bore!

A curtsy's not necessary
Unless you're meeting a queen,
But a smooth, graceful dip
Might easily be seen
As a little extra courtesy
And display of respect,
Which a young man might show
By giving his heels a small click.

Whatever you do,
Whether curtsy or bow,
The most important part of an introduction
Is how
You smile and you chat
With the hostess or host;
If you're natural and friendly
They'll judge you THE MOST!

Don't worry, however,
About the words that you say;
You can bet no one remembers
The very next day.
They've all been so worried
How they, themselves, would do
That they've spent no time at all
Worrying about you.

* * * * * *

CHAPTER II

HELLO, DOLLY!

Telephone Etiquette

If the telephone rings
And you run to answer it,
Be sure you're over five
Or your mother might have a fit.
For a phone is not something
You treat as a toy ---
It doesn't matter at all
If you're a girl or a boy.

You really shouldn't answer it
Unless you've been taught
What things you should say
And what things you should not.
You don't babble endlessly
Or giggle or spit,
And if you hang up on sister's boyfriend,
You'll surely get hit.

Just say, "Hello," and then,
"May I tell her who's calling?"
And set it down gently,
Not to sound like it's falling.
Now, go and get your mother,
Don't stand there and shout;
For all you know, for a moment,
She might have stepped out.

Or if she's not there
But a sitter is home,
Explain that to the person
On the end of the phone.
If you're asked to take a message,
Make sure it's real neat;
If you don't understand,
Say, "Would you please repeat?"

✳ ✳ ✳ ✳ ✳ ✳

Always say, "Goodbye,"
When you've finished a chat;
It's like ending a visit
By putting on your hat.

Tell Mom not to let
Baby talk on the phone;
She might find it cute,
But she'll be quite alone.
Other people don't enjoy
Baby's gurgles and goos.
Don't let it happen again,
Instead take my cues.

Don't dial a strange number
Just for something to do.
You might reach an old lady on crutches
Who

Has to hobble 'cross the room
Just to answer the phone,
Only to find when she gets there
That it's just the dial tone.

And in her haste to answer it,
She might slip and lie
On the floor all alone
'Til someone hears her feeble cry.
And the person who made the call
Just couldn't care less...
He's already planning
How to cause someone else stress.

* * * * * *

A phone is not to be used
To play tricks or cause strife;
When properly used,
It can even help save a life.

CHAPTER III

BEST MANNERS <u>AND</u> BEST CLOTHES?

It's a Party!

"Oh boy!" "Goody, goody!" or
"Hot dog!" you shout
When you open your mailbox,
Reach in and bring out
A large colored envelope
Addressed in ink oh-so-bright,
Inviting you to a party
Next Saturday night.

Check with your parents, of course,
To make sure you can go,
Then call the host RIGHT AWAY,
Just as soon as you know.
Don't EVER wait until
The very last hour,
Then show up unexpected,
Right out of the shower.

If the invitation you receive
Doesn't mention what to wear,
Such as "play clothes," "party clothes,"
Or "anything but bare,"
Don't hesitate to call your host
And ask for his advice.
When you're going to a party,
You want to look really nice.

If you show up in a fancy dress
Or a real cool coat and tie,
And find everyone else in jeans or shorts ---
Oh dear, couldn't you just DIE?

I know, for I've been through it all
And though I did survive,
The night of that very awful event
I wished I were not alive.

It is a compliment to the host
That you care about your dress,
And being attired properly
Will save a lot of stress.
So don't forget to call your host
Or have your mother call his,
And then you'll know whether to "fancy up"
Or just to come "as is."

* * * * * *

If it's a birthday party
To which you're invited,
Hope your best friend goes, too,
That he isn't slighted.
Be sure that the gift
Which you take to your friend
Is something he'll like,
Not some old odd or end.

However, if your invitation reads,
"No presents, please,"
Don't take one, it's not expected
And might make others ill at ease.
If you want to treat your friend,
Take a gift on another day,
Or take him out for ice cream
And tell him grandly, "I'll pay!"

* * * * * *

Give your gift to the birthday person
Upon your arrival,
And play nicely with the others ---
It will ensure your survival.
But if you are rude
And you shove and you push,
It will be your own fault
If you end up on your tush.

If hot dogs or hamburgers
Are the fare at the party
(You might get tea sandwiches
Which aren't quite so hearty),

I suggest you forgo
Runny catsup and mustard,
Lest they end up in your lap
Like a sloppy cup custard.

* * * * * *

When it's time to leave the party
Be sure to thank your host,
And also tell his mother
That as a hostess she's the most!
"Thank you so much, Mrs. Maupin,
I had a lovely time,
And I'm delighted that you honored
Your son who just turned nine."

* * * * * *

Take your own favors home,
Not those of the others.
It would be nice if you'd share
With your sisters and brothers.
Tell them the story
Of the fun that you had
And how they might have been invited
If they hadn't been bad.

CHAPTER IV

OH, NO! DO I HAVE TO?

Thank You Notes and the Written Word

No one wants to write
Thank you notes any more,
But if you do you'll stick out
Like a thumb that is sore.
And mothers will be so impressed
By your pen
That you'll be invited back
Again and again.

The note that you write
Needn't be very wordy,
Just make sure that your penmanship
Appears to be sturdy.
Use only the words
That you know how to spell,
And of which you are certain
Of the meaning as well.

For a pal's special party,
Thank you notes go in pairs:
One for your friend,
One for the mother who cares.
Thank them each
For the lovely time that you had,
And for the refreshments they served
(Even if they were bad).

Than add "Very sincerely,"
With your name down below;
Address it and stamp it
And away it will go.

* * * * * *

For birthdays or Christmas
When you get lots of presents,
You really must write
To the person who sent it.
Whether it's Grandpa or Aunt
Or old Uncle Joe,

Just write and say, "Thanks,"
To make sure that they know
Their gift arrived safely
Through rain, snow or sleet,
And the ball or the bat or the doll's
Really neat.

If you ever receive
A card that says, "Honey,
I just wanted to send you
A little extra money,"
Be sure you send thanks
So next year they'll send more,
Which they certainly won't
If their gift you ignore.

* * * * * *

When you have to write a thank you note,
Don't ever buy a card
That has "Thank You" printed on it
And think it won't be hard

'Cause all you do is sign your name;
That really isn't fair.
Someone bought and wrapped a special gift,
Writing a note is just your share.

✳   ✳   ✳   ✳   ✳   ✳

If you have to write a letter
To a neighbor or a friend,
Be sure it's addressed properly
Before you stamp and send.

To a boy who's under nine,
You would address the lad as "Master,"
And when he reaches 18,
It is "Mr." forever after.
In between those ages,
You would use only his name,
But use the title when proper
So it will not seem so plain.

Until she is through high school,
A young lady's known as "Miss,"
And after that it's "Ms."
Even if she is your sis.

Married ladies are called "Mrs."
But it's "Ms." when on the job,
But "Mrs." when they're married,
Even if it's to the Mob.

There are some older ladies
Who have never had a beau;
They've tried and tried and tried
But it has just never been so.
Ladies like Aunt Tillie
Or your teacher, Miss Greengage,
Will be forever known as "Miss,"
More in keeping with their age.

MISS   MS.   MRS.   MISS

If your neighbors both are doctors,
Do you know how to address them?
Dr. John Brown's on the line above
And Dr. Jane Brown down below him.
Or use "The Doctors Brown,"
Which also would be quite proper,
But never "Dr. and Mrs.",
Even if their name is Hopper.

Dr. John Brown
 and Dr. Jane Brown
1721 Park Ave.
NY, NY 10014

If you use the title "Dr."
Before the name of a friend,
Then don't use "M.D." after it...
Dr. John Brown...that's the end.

Dr. John Brown
203 Main St.
Ann Arbor, MI 48108

When a friend or a relative
Passes away,
You must write a note...
Do you know what to say?

"Dear Aunt Alice:
I was so very sorry to hear
Uncle George passed away
A little earlier this year.
He was a favorite of mine,
Full of jokes and good cheer,
And always so gentle;
I was glad he lived near.
I enjoyed being with him
And will miss him a lot,
But at least, dear Aunt Alice,
You I've still got."

What you want her to know
During this period of grief,
Is that your thoughts are with her;
Be kind but be brief.

CHAPTER V

MOUTHING OFF

Grammar and The Spoken Word

The way that you speak
Is a good indication
Of the use you are making
Of your education.
You'll be much better thought of
If your grammar is proper.
You might even impress
That stuck-up name dropper.

* * * * * *

It is never <u>an</u> historic place
Or a city;
All the newscasters say that, my dears,
What a pity.
You only use <u>an</u>
When the "h" is silent,
But of course it is nothing
About which to get violent.

You say <u>an</u> hour of time
Or <u>an</u> honor it would be
If the lovely Princess Di
Should invite you to tea.
But it's <u>a</u> history book
Or <u>a</u> historic occasion,
Never <u>an</u> historical weekend,
That's an abrasion.

Reporters on TV
Just can't get this right,
Not only when they speak,
But probably when they write.
But, now <u>you know</u>
So be smug in your knowledge;
You are right
And you haven't yet been to college!

* * * * * *

Nothing ever happens
<u>Between you and I</u>;
If I remembered the reason,
I'd gladly tell you why.
I just know that it's only
<u>Between you and me</u>...

Oh, I know the reason;
It's 'cause I'm older than thee!

No one ever <u>takes</u> you and <u>I</u>
Out to lunch,
Or even <u>takes</u> you and <u>I</u>
Out to brunch.
But they'd be delighted
To <u>take</u> you and <u>me</u>;
It's just that they'd never
<u>Take I</u>, don't you see?

And they'd never <u>give</u>
Katie and <u>I</u> a present,
Even at Christmas time
And if they had sent it.
But they'd love to give one
<u>To</u> Katie and <u>me</u>,
Just never <u>to I</u>.
Again, don't you see?

Would you ever say,
"Mother's <u>taking I</u> to a movie"?
Of course not,
Even if your mother were groovy.

So why would you say,
"Mom's <u>taking</u> David and <u>I</u>"?
I certainly don't know,
Can you please tell me why?

✳ ✳ ✳ ✳ ✳ ✳

If you say, "I <u>could</u> care less,"
What you're saying is that you care,
But what you mean is just the opposite,
Of that you must be aware.
So say, "I <u>couldn't</u> care less,"
Which gets the message across
That you really do not care at all,
Then give your head a toss.

✳ ✳ ✳ ✳ ✳ ✳

Let's divide this banana
Just <u>between</u> you and me.
When someone else comes along,
It will be <u>among</u> us three.
If only two are involved,
You would use "between,"
But if more, it's "among,"
Like you, me, and Maureen.

CHAPTER VI

KNIVES AND FORKS AND SPOONS, OH MY!

Setting a Table

When setting a table
There is only <u>one</u> <u>way</u>,
Which you're going to learn now,
On this very day.

* * * * * *

You start with the plate,
Set it right in the middle;
Knives next, to the right,
That's no longer a riddle.
Be sure the sharp edge
Is put facing the plate;
Now, next comes the soup spoon,
See...isn't this great?
The soup spoon is placed
Beyond the knives to the right...
I want you to learn this
If it takes you all night.

All of your forks go
On the left side only,
Except seafood cocktail,
Farthest right, very lonely.
The dinner fork goes next
To the big plate so pretty,
Then the salad fork...
While working, why not sing a ditty?

Farthest left, for the napkin,
You now are quite ready.
Be sure that you place it
With a hand that's real steady;
You don't want to cover
The forks which you've placed.
Everything one inch away from the edge
Should be spaced.

Your salad plate is left
Beyond the utensils,
All glasses to the right
Lined up straight as pencils;
Except for the champagne,
Which is set a little behind

And is served only with dessert...
I hope you don't mind.

When using a plate
For your butter and bread,
It goes above the forks,
Right there, straight ahead.

This is a very formal,
European-type setting,
Which shows, by their placement,
That you are getting

Your salad served after your entree,
For as you can see,
Your salad utensils are not
Where they ordinarily would be.

* * * * * *

Salt and Peppers:
A small set for each person is nice
But if that is not possible,
Don't even think twice.
It would be smart though
To use two or more sets;
They're easier to reach,
More convenient to get.

If you want to use candles,
Don't forget this advice:
Never light them during the daytime
Though you think it is nice.
It is only after dark
They are properly lighted.
The ladies will love them
Since all their flaws will be slighted.

Now flowers in the middle
And you're really all set.
Make them low enough to see over,
Please don't forget.
And when you grow up,
At no matter what else you are able,
One thing will be certain...
You can set a fine table.

Don't set the table
With items you're not going to use;
It gives your friends
Too many choices to choose.

* * * * * *

The teaspoon, as a utensil,
Is greatly overrated;
It's not all that important
Even if it's silverplated.
To be used very properly,
It is brought in with the cup
On the saucer with the coffee or the tea
After you sup.

It should not be in the lineup
Of utensils by the plate
For you use it just for stirring,
Not for something that you ate.

INFORMAL SETTING

For eating there's a soup spoon,
And a spoon for the dessert,
Which goes above the dinner plate,
Just ask the butler, Bert.
However, this is only done at meals
That are more formal;
A teaspoon set beside the knife
Is really much more normal.

* * * * * *

Still Spinning...

CHAPTER VII

E T   (Eating Tidily)

Table Manners

To hold your utensils
There is only one way,
So read this very carefully
And follow what I say.

*   *   *   *   *   *

When cutting your food,
The fork prongs are pointing down
With fingers curled 'round the handle,
It's easy, don't frown.
The index finger lays straight down
The handle of the fork;
Never clench it in your fist
Like you're stabbing your pork!

That's all with your left hand,
Provided you're right-handed.
Your right hand holds the knife
(I won't leave you stranded)
With fingers curling 'round
And index down the back.
Cut gently,
This isn't some tree you are trying to hack.

COOL   NOT!

After cutting one bite,
Lay your knife on your plate
And switch your fork to your right hand,
Hurry, don't wait.

Spear the piece with your fork
And bring to your mouth, prongs up.
Now see, you are learning
How gracefully you can sup!

Now switch the fork back
To the left hand and then,
Begin the same process
All over again.

This manner of eating
Is called the American way,
But you use so much motion
That some people say
The Continental style is better;
That's next on our list.
I'll explain it real carefully
And hope you get the gist.

* * * * * *

Hold the fork in your left hand
And the knife in your right
All through the meal,
Even if it takes you all night.

The fork prongs are now down
When bringing food up to your mouth,
(Do this properly and you'll look like
An aristocrat from the South).

AMERICAN STYLE   CONTINENTAL STYLE

The knife may be used
To push food onto the fork,
Do not use a breadstick
To do the same work.
Remember that the knife
Is always in your hand,
Unless you set it down
To pick up the glass with the fancy band.

Instead of all the switching
From hand over to hand,
You'll be eating quite smoothly
And looking quite grand.
I would advise the Continental way;
Do it without a hitch
And people will think
You are well-travelled and rich.

* * * * * *

When sitting at the table
Do not slouch down in your seat.
You sit upright all through the meal,
On the floor keep both your feet.
You bring the food up to your mouth,
Not your mouth down to the food;
Now keep this up all through the meal
And you'll be doing very good.

You may rest your arm upon the table
But only to the wrist;

Try laying it along the edge
And I will certainly resist.
No elbows on the table
Until you have finished your meal,
Then you are allowed to put them there.
How's that? Do we have a deal?

NOT!   COOL

Be aware that milk
Leaves a rim on your lip...
Use your napkin gently
And pat it a bit.
The same goes for cocoa
With whipped cream on the top,

So, again use your napkin
And give it a blot.

For anything served in a dish
With a stem,
Use your spoon, not your fork,
And if you have a yen,
Hold it ever so lightly
(To get the last dribble)
So it won't topple over
And end up on your middle.

Napkins are never
To be waved in the air
Or snapped at someone's tush,
That wouldn't be fair.
They are meant to lay neatly
In your lap for all time
Except when raised gently
To blot food or grime.
If you must leave the table,
The napkin goes on your chair

And when you return,
It should still be there.

* * * * * *

If you ever attend a party
Where the food is served buffet,
Don't ever, ever, EVER
Let me see your fingers stray
From the food upon the table
Directly to your mouth...
It would remind me of the manners
Of a big, fat, sloppy cow'th.

You take a plate into your hands
And then select your food
By circling 'round the table
And choosing what fits your mood.
Don't be a pig, take a little of each,
Then find a place to sit.
Only now that you are seated
May you start to eat a bit.

* * * * * *

When dining with friends
At any type of cafe,
They will remember how you eat
Much more than what you say.
So don't talk with your mouth full,
Keep it closed very tight,
And you'll be able to present
A much more pleasant sight.

* * * * * *

CHAPTER VIII

PIGGING OUT

How to Eat Difficult Foods

Good Grief! What is that funny looking,
Weirdo green chunk?
You certainly could never, ever
Call it a "hunk."
It looks really tough
And is covered with leaves.
What do I do with it?
Won't somebody tell me, PLEASE?

0.K. It's an Artichoke,
That is its name,
And eating it is almost
Like playing a game.
First you pull off a leaf
From the very outside
And handle it confidently,
Do it with pride.

Hold it right at the top
Between index finger and thumb.
Don't spear with your fork,
That would look really dumb.
Melted butter is usually provided
As a dip
And it is to put your leaves into,
Not to pick up and sip.

Coat the bottom half of the leaf
With the mixture that's there,
Then put in your mouth
And bite down with great care.

You properly pull the leaf out
From between your clenched teeth,
Enjoying the taste that comes with it
From the mix and the leaf.

You perform this act over
And over again
Until the big leaves are gone
And you're ready to say "when."
Now you are at the point
Where all you have left
Is a little teepee of leaves,
Remove it, be deft.

After you pull off the leaves
There's a soft little fuzz,

Like that on the baby's head,
The one they call "Buzz."
Hold the artichoke and scrape
With your knife 'til it's smooth,
For the rest, it's your knife
And your fork that you'll uthe (I lisp).

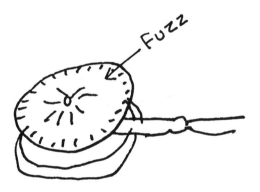

And now you have come
To the very best part - -
That delicious, nutritious
Artichoke heart!

Dip it in butter
Or whatever is there;
You've done so much work
You needn't offer to share.

So, now you are finished
And what have you got?
A plate full of leaves.
Was it worth it? I think not.

Fried chicken is ideally eaten
Out-of-doors,
Like during the summer
When you're down at the shores.
But if you're served chicken,
Whether broiled, fried, or baked
And it comes in one big piece,
Don't make the mistake
Of picking it up
If you're eating under a roof;
You don't want to make
An unnecessary goof.

Use your knife and your fork
To be really cool;
You don't want to appear to be
An uncouth fool.
First you cut off the leg
Then next comes the wing;
And after that, it's sort of
"Do your own thing."

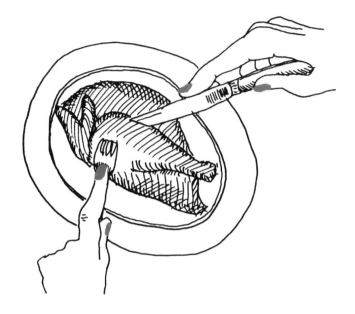

Cut off as much meat as you can
With your knife
And hope you accomplish it
Without too much strife.
Eat each bite as it's cut;
Don't save them all up
To chow down all at once---
That's too much like a pup.

* * * * * *

When eating your soup:
Tip the spoon away from you,

Then sip from the nearest side,
And when you are through,
Set your spoon on the plate
That is under your bowl,
And make sure it's secure,
That it will not roll.

But if your soup is served
In a plate low and wide,
Then it's all right
To leave your soup spoon inside.
And if the dish has handles,
You may lift it and sip,
But never if it's a bowl
With only a lip.

* * * * * *

If you're served iceberg lettuce
That comes in a wedge,
And if you've no knife,
Cut with your fork, use the edge.
And hope (even pray)
It won't scoot onto the floor:

If it does,
I suggest you head straight for the door.

* * * * * *

If watermelon's available,
Just hope that it's seedless
Or you might engage
In a fight that is needless,
And scatters seeds and saliva
To be cleaned up mañana.
You'd be better off
Just to eat a banana.

NOT!   NEAT

When eating a sandwich
That's big, fat, and greasy,
Try to be neat
Though I know it's not easy.
If you cut it in half
It's much easier to handle
And will stay on your plate,
Not fall into your sandal.

* * * * * *

Corn on the cob
Is so much fun to crunch
But it sticks to your teeth
In a real ugly bunch.
So unless you're with family
In the outdoors somewhere,
I suggest you don't eat it
For people might stare.

* * * * * *

If a stalk of asparagus
Shows up on your plate,

You'd be wise not to eat;
Look around you and wait
To see what the hostess
Will do with her portion.
She might pick it up,
Which is an acceptable motion,
Provided it's crisp.
If it's limp use your fork;
Your knife will help make it
A little less work.

* * * * * *

The roll on your plate
Is there for a reason;
You break it and butter it
(Don't use salt to season).
Just break it and butter it
And eat bite by bite,
Never all at once,
That really isn't right.

With toast it's the same,
Handle it little by little;

66

Never butter all at once,
Break it up at the middle.
The only bread buttered
Without breaking it up,
Is a biscuit or muffin
Real hot from its cup.

* * * * * *

Don't ever cut spaghetti,
It really isn't done,
Or slurp it up from plate to mouth,
Not even just in fun.
It should be twisted on your fork
Just like a young ballerina,
Especially when it is covered with
A lovely sauce Florentina.

Now noodles are something else again,
You may cut them all you want.
If a friend asks why you are doing this,
Tell him you learned from your aunt.
But the spaghetti should be twisted
On your fork in small amounts,
Like maybe five strands at a time,
But just guess, don't bother to count.

When eating a crab,
You don't want to be one.
If you know what to do,
You might even have fun.
So, pay close attention
And we'll review this together;
When you've learned how to "crack crab,"
You'll feel an awful lot better.

There are hard shells and soft shells
And some that are squished,
But we will discuss crab legs,
A favorite dish.

* * * * * *

For a hard shell, pull the legs from the body
With your fingers,
Then suck the meat out quietly,
Be sure you do not linger.
Then turn the body over,
Right onto its back
And pick the meat out with a seafood fork;
But please, don't make an attack.

Or if it's a big, fat leg
And you are given a nutcracker,
Crack it into sections,
But don't act like a linebacker.
Then use a fork or pick
To get the meat out of the shell,
Then dip it into the sauce that's served
And enjoy...you've done so well.

For a soft shell you're expected
To eat the whole crab and shell,
So use your knife and fork
And I am sure that you'll do swell.

* * * * * *

A lobster is handled
In much the same way
But it's served on its back,
"Belly up," you might say.
It also is served
With a bib for your use,
Don't tie it tightly,
Just let it hang loose.

Again, use the nutcracker
To break up the shell,
And pick out the meat
Which you now do so well.
The meat in the body
Comes out in large hunks,
So use your fork
To cut into chunks.

Now dip it in the butter
Which is served so nicely melted
And loosen that strap
Around your waist so tightly belted.
Be aware, if you eat the whole thing,
You'll regret your greed tomorrow
When you try to zip your jeans and can't,
Your heart will fill with sorrow.

CHAPTER IX

McMANNERS

Fast Food Etiquette

Before you'll feel at ease
In a fancy restaurant,
You should practice awhile
At a neighborhood haunt.
Like McDonald's or Wendy's
Or even Burger King;
After mastering those,
The Ritz will be no big thing.

No matter your age,
Try to sit very still
For there's nothing more annoying
Than children who will
Jump up and down
And race around the room,
Making the experience for all
An evening of gloom.

Don't ever play tunes with your spoons
On your glasses,
Your father might get even
And make you mow grasses.
Remember why you've gone there---
Only to dine,
Not to pinch your little sister
And listen to her whine.

And don't bang your silverware
To make a loud noise,
That is certainly no sign
Of a young person's poise.

Eat quietly;
Give your parents a chance to talk.
When you want to go out again,
I'm sure they won't balk.

When you've finished your meal,
Clean your papers up neatly
And deposit them in the trash,
But do it discreetly.

If you've had an accident
And spilled on the floor,
Ask someone to clean it up
Before you go out the door.

Be nice to the help,
They are there to assist you
And when you are older
You might want to do what they do.
If you behave nicely
And make your parents proud,
I'm sure people will notice---
You'll stand out in the crowd.

* * * * * *

Still Spinning...

CHAPTER X

SPECIAL OCCASIONS

Very Nice Restaurant Etiquette

Follow the man in the tux
When he leads to your table,
And smile when he pulls out your chair
To enable
You to sit down.
Then lift your napkin so ample
But only after the hostess
Has set an example.

"Oh my, goodness gracious,
Just look at that table,"
You gasp as you wonder
If you'll ever be able
To sort out all those knives
And those forks and those spoons;
Most of them simple,
But some with Gadroons.

But don't get upset,
It's really quite easy
(Don't check out the spoons,
I'm sure they're not greasy).
You start on the outside
And work your way in,
So that soup spoon you see
Is where you begin.

All knives and all spoons
Are placed to your right,
All forks to your left
In the soft candlelight.
Your napkin and salad plate
And butter plate, too,
Are also on the left side
Just waiting for you.

* * * * * *

Always watch your hostess
To see what to do,
To be checked out during a meal
To her is not new.

But try to be subtle;
Don't gawk and don't stare,
Just notice her quietly
And keep yourself aware.

Most often your napkin
Is on the left side,
But sometimes you'll find it
Like bunny ears tied.
Of course this is done
By people with nothing else to do:
(I'm too busy making the world
A better place for you).

But napkins, very properly,
Can be right in the middle
And you can admire the table
While the man with the fiddle
Plays your favorite tune
While you're waiting to dine
On this very special occasion
When you're finally nine.

GLASS TURNED DOWN   NO THANK YOU!

Of course you'll refuse
If you're offered some wine,
Just say, "No thank you,"
That is perfectly fine.
Don't turn your glass over
So it sits upside down,
And don't put your hand over it ---
That merits a frown.

All beverages: water glasses
And wine glasses bright,

As well as your coffee cup,
Appear to your right.
Though glasses are always lined up
When you're seated,
Coffee cups or cocoa
Don't appear until needed.

* * * * * *

Try to order foods
That are easiest to eat,
So instead of being sloppy,
You can be really neat.
Your mom will be happy
You did not stain your clothes,
And it's Mother, not Father,
Who best really knows.

* * * * * *

Don't pick up the money
You see left on the table,
That's only for the waiter
And allows him to be able

To pay for his acting class,
Which is training him to be
Another Tom Cruise
Or a big star on TV.

Did you know that all foods
Are served to your left side?
And all beverages are poured from the right,
Don't try to hide.
You might lean a bit
One way or the other,
To help the waiter do his job ---
You'll get thanks from his mother.

* * * * * *

CHAPTER XI

NOT HOME ALONE

Houseguesting

Oh, how exciting!
What a wonderful sensation
When your best friend invites you
On her family's vacation!
You'll be going to the mountains
For two wonderful, long weeks
And you can already imagine
Climbing all those craggy peaks.

Be sure you take your hostess
A gift that's really dandy
Like a big tin of popped popcorn
Or a lovely box of candy.
Always mind your manners
And do everything they ask,
Especially when it's helping out
With some dull household task.

NOT!   WELCOME!

Don't borrow your friend's sweater
That you pulled out of a drawer.
She might get so upset she'd throw
All your clothes on the floor.
And don't ever go sneaking 'round
And snooping through her stuff;
Explaining why you're doing so
Would be awfully, awfully tough.

* * * * * *

It would be very nice of you
To take your hosts to dinner
At a restaurant of their choice---
That would really make you a winner.

Tell them your parents insisted
That this should be your treat,
Then tell the waiter to give <u>you</u> the check;
They'll think you are really neat.

Or give your host your money
And ask him to pay the bill,
Including enough to cover the tip,
Which I'm certain that you will.
Fifteen percent is enough
If you're at a hamburger chain,
But twenty percent is expected
If a Ritz-Carlton is your aim.

* * * * * *

Of course you'll always make your bed
And <u>offer</u> to do boring chores,
Although you'd much rather be hiking
In the glorious outdoors.
Always ask permission
Before you use their phone
Or they might get upset with you
And leave you HOME ALONE!

It is never, ever easy
To be a perfect guest,
But remember this is <u>their</u> house
And do what they request.

* * * * * *

CHAPTER XII

ETC.

Things I Know that You Probably Don't but I'm Willing to Share

Of course you are familiar
With that age-old Golden Rule;
Of all the ancient guidelines,
That really is a jewel.
So follow its advice
And to your friends be always kind,
But remember most of all
That it's your Mother you should mind.

* * * * * *

I, myself, can't understand
Why some people are so rude.
To make someone unhappy...
Does that make you feel good?
You will find when you are older
There are other things in life

That are much more rewarding
Than always causing strife.
You won't be very popular
If you are always rude;
Much better it is to give a high five
And say, "Cowabunga, Dude!"

* * * * * *

Don't ever make fun
Of someone in a wheelchair.
You have no idea
Of what might have put him there.
The same thing could probably
Happen to you,
And if somebody stared,
Wouldn't that make you blue?

If you ever meet someone
Who talks with a stutter,
Please don't say, "Speak up!
I can't hear you! Don't mutter!"
For that would be mean
And her face would turn red

And she might start to cry
And wish she were dead.

* * * * * *

There are five little words
That are an absolute must
To have in your vocabulary---
Don't you DARE let them rust!
Do you have any idea
Of what they might be?
"Thank you" are two of them,
Now there are only three.
"Excuse me" are another two
And that leaves only one
Which, of course, is "Please,"
Without which you won't get much done.

They are all easy to spell
And very simple to say.
Use them often
And you'll make someone's day.

Don't think you're real cool
Using four letter words;
That kind of logic
Is strictly for the birds.
Everyone's heard them before,
They're really old hat,
And if you can't shock somebody,
Then what fun is that?

* * * * * *

All folks are created equal;
Whether you come from near or afar
God saw no difference at all in us,
He loves us for what we are.
There are tall folks, short ones, old ones,
And others who are fatter;
But since everyone is different,
Then differences shouldn't matter.

* * * * * *

The new kids in your class
Are totally awesome,
So be sure when they're reciting
You don't giggle or yawn some,

For it's not polite to be noisy
And it makes you look bad
When you'd rather impress them
And be thought really rad.

✳   ✳   ✳   ✳   ✳   ✳

Now it's time to deal
With that noisy, wet sneeze.
Hurry! Turn your head away,
Use a tissue, PLEASE!
Don't EVER cough or sneeze
In someone's face or on their food.
It's difficult to imagine
Any action quite as rude.

And don't you dare even THINK
Of blowing your nose
In your napkin, a towel,
Or especially your clothes!
If your nose drips so bad
And it runs all day long,
In bed drinking juices
Is where you belong.

How boring life would be for us
If everyone you knew
Were the exact same color you are,
That very special hue.
So there are people who are black or red
And people who are white,
Which should make everyone happy
And everything all right.
Unfortunately there are some folks
Who think that this is bad;
How much easier it would be for us
If we'd all been born plaid.

CONGRATULATIONS!

Now that you've finished,
Don't you think that you ought
To go out and practice
What you have been taught?

A web has been woven
Which will be hard to break,
For now you know how to act
And won't make a mistake...

Will you?

The bottom line
Of having good manners
Is to make other people
Feel nice.
So study this book
Again and again,
And please, PLEASE
Take its advice.

INDEX